# Gunner Stahl
# Portraits

I HAVE SO MUCH TO TELL YOU

*Gunner Stahl*

ABRAMS IMAGE, NEW YORK

Editor: Garrett McGrath
Designer: Heesang Lee, Gunner Stahl, Brian Wright, Chris Jennings
Production Manager: Michael Kaserkie

Library of Congress Control Number: 2019930876
ISBN: 978-1-4197-4131-9
eISBN: 978-1-68335-796-4
B&N Exclusive Edition ISBN: 978-1-4197-4442-6
Urban Outfitters Exclusive Edition ISBN: 978-1-4197-4526-3

Printed and bound in the United States
10 9 8 7 6 5 4 3 2 1

Abrams Image books are available at special discounts
when purchased in quantity for premiums and promotions
as well as fundraising or educational use. Special editions
can also be created to specification. For details, contact
specialsales@abramsbooks.com or the address below.

Abrams Image® is a registered trademark of Harry N. Abrams, Inc.

**ABRAMS** The Art of Books
195 Broadway, New York, NY 10007
abramsbooks.com

SIX DEGREES CREATIVE
sixxdgrs.com

In 2013, when there were blogs and I was a blogger, Gunner guessed my Gmail correctly and cold emailed me a Tumblr link to a Two-9 video he'd codirected. I responded like a jerk: "This is a personal email address. Please remove me from your mailing list." At the time, people would hit me for favors constantly, via official channels and everywhere else. On that day, I was clearly feeling the stress and taking it out on someone I didn't know. All these years later, feeling bad about my response still reminds me that when I'm in a bad mood I can say less. I'm glad it wasn't the last time we spoke.

We met a couple of years later, when I was editing *FADER* and he showed up at our office by surprise. He had lunch with one of our best writers, our social media editor took his photo, and we realized we had some mutual friends. He was sort of shy, sitting on my couch, asking nothing in particular of anyone. He seemed easy with people but hard to parse. A big part of the joy of his photos is that they tell on him. If it ever feels like he's holding back IRL, the pictures he makes are generous and excited.

Gunner's photos have eye contact, unexpected gestures, and affectionate smiles—they make emotional connections. He has a point of view, which, at least sometimes, is that his friends are champs who should be taken seriously. It looks like he loves getting to know people. In my experience this is true. Gunner tries to spend time with people who care about what they do, people he thinks have good intentions for him, and people he can learn from. He's funny and you can't really pay him to do wack shit. His photos have helped fans know artists better, and probably helped some artists know themselves better, too.

One night in Atlanta, I learned that Gunner lost his mom when he was young. My understanding is that she was really nice, a choir director who was a selfless parent and friend. I imagine she'd be more than delighted that Gunner still loves taking pictures and does it mostly by being as humane with people as possible. That night, Future was performing and we were waiting in a basement for a while, sitting across from Zaytoven, who had ridiculous, amazing boots on. I think Gunner got a photo of them.

All of us are older now. We've lost some people. Music, tech, and photography have evolved in a million chaotic ways. Everything has become less precious and our attention is fried. Having friends who aren't jerks, who can meet deadlines, and who are up-front about what they don't know is more valuable than ever. For everyone's sake, I hope Gunner gets every chance to keep learning the things he wants to learn.

**NAOMI ZEICHNER**

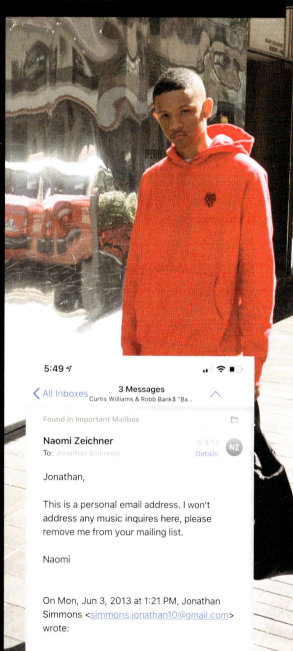

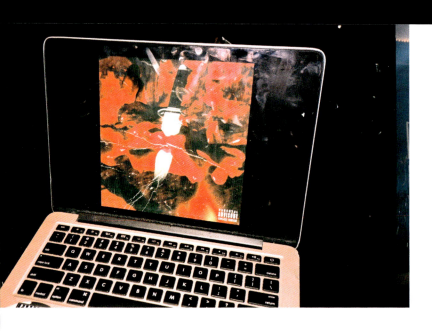

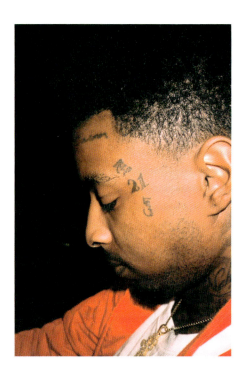

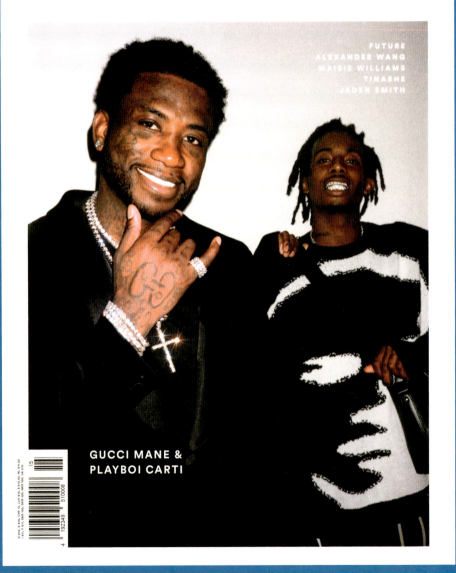

# HIGHSNOBIETY

15
FALL/WINTER 2017

FUTURE
ALEXANDER WANG
MAISIE WILLIAMS
TINASHE
JADEN SMITH

**GUCCI MANE &
PLAYBOI CARTI**

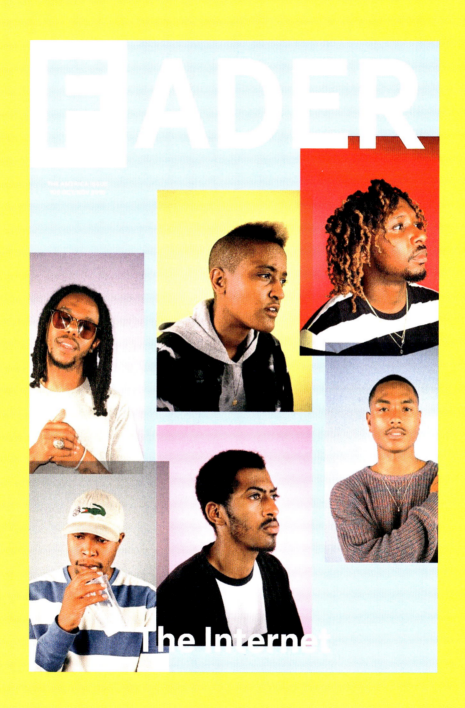

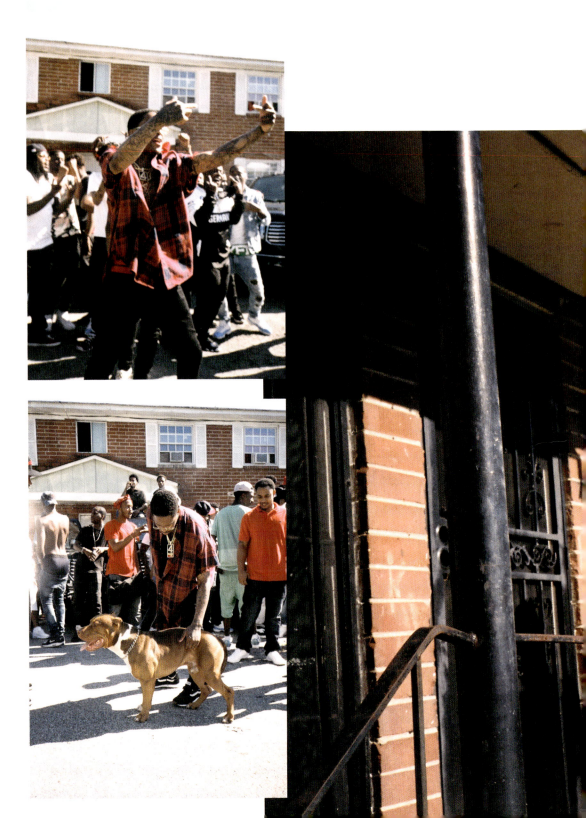

**CHI MODU**

As somebody that's been out here doing it for a long time, you can tell the difference when people are sort of faking it and when they have the passion for it. Photography is not a quick path. I could tell by the way you move that I sense you get that. It's like you receive some of the hype that comes with the generation but you have to see beyond that, you know what I mean?

**GUNNER STAHL**

Yeah, I'm in this for twenty or thirty years. I'm not in it for right now. That doesn't drive you to become better.

**CHI MODU**

Exactly. And it doesn't stay. In some ways like, they're just looking for a look or a style or your name or something like that. Ultimately, I'm safer if you're looking at my pictures and not me because my pictures keep me safe, you know what I mean? Because I can hide behind my pictures. That's always been my approach and it's tricky, you know? Because early on when you're doing that, people don't really get it, right? They're like, "How come you're not here? How come you're not shooting all these albums?" I didn't really do a whole lot of albums. You can probably kind of tell from my pictures. I didn't—I wasn't, like, the go-to for a lot of that paid work, because that work stayed within a certain community, if you understand my drift.

**GUNNER STAHL**

Yeah. It's—it's just crazy that you're telling me this, because this is the same thing that I've experienced for the last four years now.

**CHI MODU**

I'm not surprised. And you know how I can tell too, because I knew early on you were a little bit different. It's crazy. Even in four years, you've seen it right? And . . .

**GUNNER STAHL**

Even within months, I've seen it. You know, everything's so fast now. Like, it's *[snaps fingers]*.

**CHI MODU**

I mean, I remember when a Timbaland beat drove the world. I remember when Sisqo was crushing it. When I was doing it, I was doing magazine covers back when a magazine mattered, right?

**GUNNER STAHL**

Yes, when all you had was print, and that was the only way you were getting your information.

**CHI MODU**

Exactly right. And it was the only way to really feel it beyond album artwork, which you don't even really see now because of the Spotify and streaming stuff. I was shooting for editorial platforms. That's why my pictures have an editorial lean to them because I wanted my pictures to be honest and to stay.

**GUNNER STAHL**

I used to just run around music festivals or backstage at shows. But since January of last year, I took a trip to Paris, and then I was like, "Yo, I don't want to do anything like what I've been doing before." I want everything to have a more editorial look.

**CHI MODU**

I could only imagine what it's like to roll into a photo shoot for Migos. The size of the clothing rack must be massive. I was kind of notorious for no stylist. The reason why is because, they would sometimes annoy me because it would break up the flow and my connection with my subject. It can actually move you away from the actual person. It's a fine line you walk, because not everybody looks good on their own. Some people need help, you know what I mean? Even Tupac for example, he has no shirt on and tank tops in my photographs because I asked him to take the shirt off. The shirt he wore was corny. I was like, "No, man." So, he took it off, and that's why this stuff looks timeless, you know what I mean?

Whatever situation we're in, that's what we deal with, because that's part of our creative process. That's my photo background, being a photojournalist and a documentarian. When you look at my pictures, I want you to be able to look back in time and really feel like you were there.

**GUNNER STAHL**

That's the thing. Hip hop drives literally everything now.

**CHI MODU**

I didn't do a whole lot of album covers or music videos. Today, both of those facts work to my advantage. At the time people were wondering, "Oh, you're shooting pictures. Why aren't you doing videos?" Almost like that's the next step up. And not realizing that no, the destination is actually still photography. No one remembers moving. People remember stills.

**GUNNER STAHL**
I vividly remember the first photo I ever saw from you was when Big and Craig Mack got signed.

**CHI MODU**
The Bad Boy Big Mack ad. That was the first Bad Boy ad.

**GUNNER STAHL**
Oh, wow.

**CHI MODU**
Once they started becoming Bad Boy, then Puffy wanted Annie Leibovitz or Mary Ellen Mark to photograph him and J-Lo. You feel me? My community has this built-in need to be accepted by the other community. People like me aren't good enough in their minds, but it's a product of oppression. I understand it. That's why I never got called for anything. Not one Hennessy ad, not one Reebok campaign. The only albums I did were because of the artists. Snoop made sure of it. Method Man asked me. And the art director couldn't stand it—they were mad that I was shooting the Method Man album. They tried to put me in check during it because people aren't used to a black person with that kind of power in a creative setting. They would scramble for any photographer in any other complexion rather then me. I knew I was good and I knew I had the pictures, so I was like, "All right. I'll take a break and pull away from this for a bit."

I was able to license my photographs and generate some income from that while keeping a fairly low profile for over a decade. One day about six years ago I was like, "Uh-uh. They're gonna remember me." I was in New York City and saw a billboard. I was like, "You know what, I need one of those" I called up the company. I saw the number. I said, "How much does it cost for a billboard?" The guy goes, "Who are you?" I said, "I'm an artist, you know, I just want to know—" He said, "Oh, yeah? We work with artists sometimes. What's your name? Would you like to come in?" I said, "No problem." And I know once I give people my name and then they Google me, they realize my level. I went on to do a deal for six billboards. Three in Manhattan, three in Brooklyn. And I didn't have any money, really. I just worked it out. I did some photo shooting, gave them a print, and just paid a little bit of cash.

I wasn't selling anything with the billboards. And that threw people off, because I wasn't looking for work. I was looking to put my work in your face, make you deal with who the hell I was and who I am. That was my mission. Then the museum in Finland caught wind of it and they wanted to give me a career retrospective. That's how UNCATGORIZED project was born with a mission to take the art directly to the people. Bypass all middle men and blockers.

*FADER* would mess with you. *FADER* wouldn't mess with me at all.

**GUNNER STAHL**
I literally ran in *FADER*'s building in 2014. Nobody invited me. I just looked up names of editors online, I walked in the building and I was at a desk. And then I was just like, "Yo. Like, there's something I really want to do. I don't know. It might not be now, it might be later." And then eventually it just—it happened.

**CHI MODU**
I mean, you're driven. You've been driven. You've been driven for a while. You know? You got to have drive in this path. And you got it. Hey man, I want to let you know that when I reached out to you about doing something together a couple of years ago, all I really wanted to do was to have this conversation with you. You know what I mean? And kind of let you know that I see you. I know what you're doing. I know what this is. You're not alone.

We lost a lot of soldiers along the way like Tupac, Biggie, Mac Miller, and Nipsey Hussle. And it's not stopping, you know? These pictures are helping, though. They just help.

**GUNNER STAHL**
I'm just trying my hardest. Thank you for saying that. That really means a lot.

**CHI MODU**
It's the truth. And that's why I'll always encourage you to think about the creative process, you know, think about the long-term. Don't let short-term battles distract you. I need to head back now.

**GUNNER STAHL**
I appreciate you putting your meeting on hold for this. It means a lot. Thank you so much.

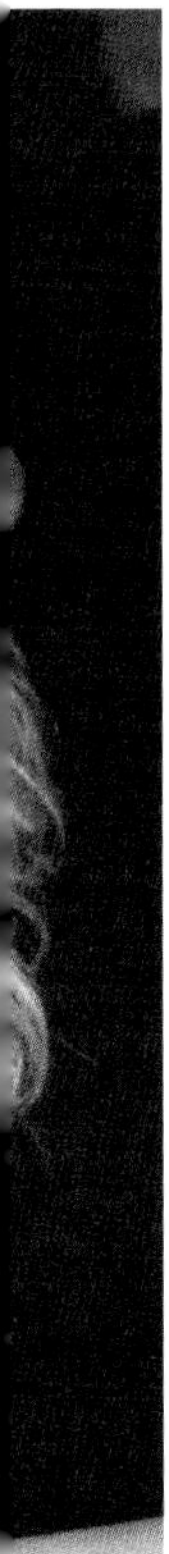

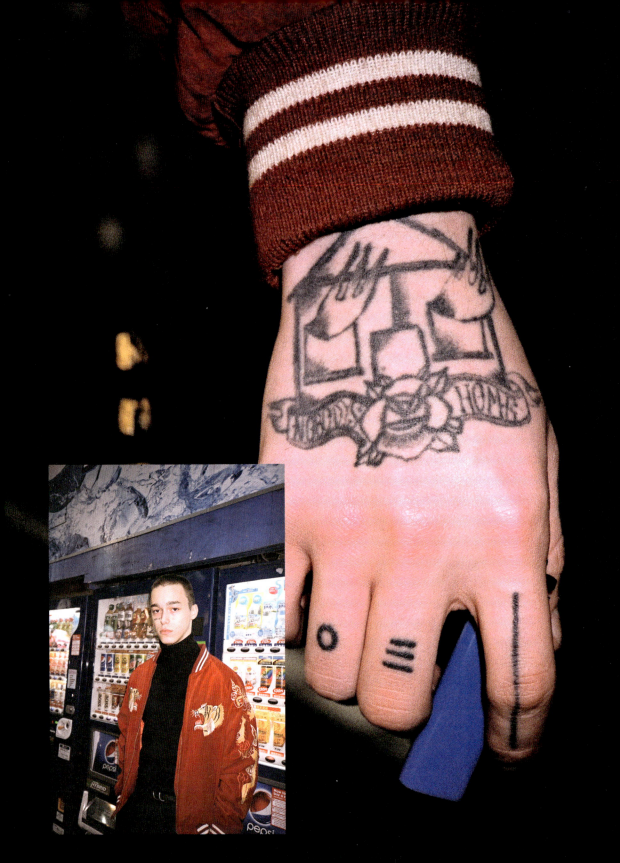

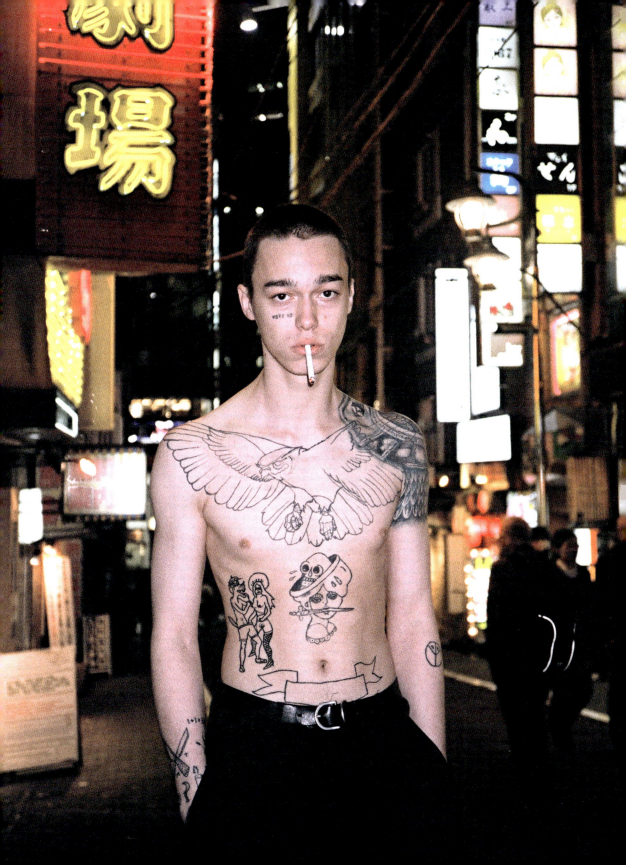

**GUNNER STAHL**
What's up?

**SWAE LEE**
Been chilling, man.

**GUNNER STAHL**
In Russia?

**SWAE LEE**
Yeah.

**GUNNER STAHL**
Man, I wish I would'a known earlier, I would've came there. I always wanted to go there.

**SWAE LEE**
Bro, I ain't gonna lie, I didn't want to come here, but this shit is fucking amazing, bro.

**GUNNER STAHL**
That's your first time over there?

**SWAE LEE**
Yeah, it's my first time here. Like, this shit is not what I thought. I thought it was gonna be hella racist, cold, and boring. But it's just the exact opposite.

**GUNNER STAHL**
But they love, like, hip-hop out there. The reason I wanted you to be a part of this is just because our careers started at the same time.

**SWAE LEE**
For real, though. We started from the starting point. Both of us just skyrocketed. Like, you really the only cameraman living like a fucking rapper and shit. You literally live a rap lifestyle.

**GUNNER STAHL**
I'm trying to. I'm really trying to. Your growth has been just so inspiring.

**SWAE LEE**
Thank you, Herc.

**GUNNER STAHL**
It's insane. I know we don't see each other a lot but I really appreciated when you said I deserved a Nobel Peace Prize for making the violence freeze for a moment in time.

**SWAE LEE**
Right, real shit, bro. They froze, right?

**GUNNER STAHL**
That's one of the most amazing things I've still to this day ever read. And I was telling people that, I was posting it. It was so amazing that you even thought to say that.

**SWAE LEE**
We got our own movement.

**GUNNER STAHL**
We actually did this. That's insane. That's very beautiful.

**SWAE LEE**
It's powerful. Even because the song went number one, we started a whole another wave for hip-hop artists.

**GUNNER STAHL**
New rock stars.

**SWAE LEE**
Real shit.

**GUNNER STAHL**
You proved that this shit is bigger than everything that's around us, bro. Shit's crazy.

**SWAE LEE**
For real. Ain't no limit to what we can do that, man.

**GUNNER STAHL**
There's absolutely no limit. Let me see. What should I ask you first? Jacob said you had some questions. I was gonna ask about what you remember from your early career in 2014.

**SWAE LEE**
Man, just like shit. Being in Atlanta, making my first, like, two thousand dollars in a club. Just going—literally niggas fighting and went on, like, building tours and venue tours. And nigga was all like, ratshit hood club tours.

**GUNNER STAHL**
Man, I went with y'all. I remember y'all picking me up from my grandmother's house. I hopped in the van with y'all. We went to Mississippi to some random club. Then drove from Mississippi to Miami, which was, like, fourteen hours. Then we went back to Mississippi.

**SWAE LEE**
In the van! Oh shit, bro, you was with us, man!

**GUNNER STAHL**
See? That's what I'm saying. That's why I wanted to talk to you about all of this. I wasn't there for everything, but I remember when Mike first introduced me to y'all. I remember everything. I just remember believing, "oh yes, this is it." Like, this energy is unmatched.

**SWAE LEE**
For reals.

**GUNNER STAHL**

Exactly. I remember when I first heard "We." Mike played me "We," and I was like, this energy can't even be categorized, like, right now, bro. Because it's just something completely brand-new. But we went from Mississippi to Miami back to Mississippi then back to Atlanta.

**SWAE LEE**

Wow.

**GUNNER STAHL**

Do you remember anything about that time period?

**SWAE LEE**

Hell, yeah. Like, life was transitioning. Like, my whole life was transitioning slowly but surely. It just kept leveling up and more people kept recognizing us and what we was doing and, just like, the prices of everything we was doing was going up. Like, you know what I'm saying? It's not even about proving ourselves, because we knew we were—we was on and what we were capable of, but we had to get across some barriers, you know what I'm saying? So it was just like—it was like nonstop grind, nigga. No sleep, thinking about what's the next song. Like, sometimes, like we'll be dropping next videos, where we going next. I got two questions for you. Have you ever taken a picture upside-down?

**GUNNER STAHL**

Lol, na I don't think I have.

**SWAE LEE**

Have you ever shot yourself?

**GUNNER STAHL**

I'd have to be on real drugs to ever take a picture of myself. I've taken photos with the lens cap on though, and they came out straight black. I left the cap on the first time I ever shot 21 Savage. None of the photos came out. I was convinced he was a vampire before I realized the lens cap was on. You guys are performing at Wireless this week. You remember last year at Wireless when you smashed the two bottles together?

**SWAE LEE**

Yes, we shot that 42 video. You told me not to do that. Everyone did. You were right. That shit almost cut my vein. I could have died.

**GUNNER STAHL**

I remember the medics wrapping your wrist like twenty times and in the middle of you perform-ing I saw the blood still soaking through the wraps. I was scared for you for a second.

**SWAE LEE**

My wrist hurts right now just thinking about it. I almost passed out. I remember during the performance thinking, "Damn, am I gonna make it through?"

**GUNNER STAHL**

You even stayed after, I was so surprised.

**SWAE LEE**

I had to it, it was lit. Everybody around was lit. Man, you've really changed photography.

**GUNNER STAHL**

Thank you, man.

**SWAE LEE**

A lot of people say that they are inspired by you or that they shoot film because of you.

**GUNNER STAHL**

Thank you, bro. I feel like I've done nothing but simply made it such a private thing.

138

YOU HAVE TO TAKE A S
TO REALIZE HOW TO
FORWARD. IT'S SO EASY
LOST NOW, BUT REGAR
NEVER BE AFRAID OF
AT YOUR LOW POINT.
OF ALL OF THAT
REMEMBER DEEP BREA
MEANT TO BE HELD

A MESSAGE FR
Nick Hol

## INDEX